Battling the Beast – Through the power of prayer

By
Larry Mondragon

Co-Editor
Floyd Mondragon

Battling the Beast – Through the power of prayer

Copyright @ 2023 by Larry Mondragon

All rights reserved. No part of this book may be reproduced, distributed, or transmitted in any form or by any means, including photocopying, recording, or other electronic or mechanical methods, without the prior written permission of the publisher, except in the case of brief quotations embodied in critical reviews and certain other noncommercial uses permitted by copyright law.

Battling the Beast – Through the power of prayer

By: Larry Mondragon
Co-Editor: Floyd Mondragon

Printed in the United States of America

Dedication

To my wife, Mary Mondragon

Introduction

If someone asked me the question If you can summarize your life, at least so far, in a few words, what would you say?" I would have to think a bit, but would probably say, being a fighter. Not the type of fighter that gets into a ring and uses his fists to win a boxing match, but I am the type of fighter that strives every day to make something of myself.

I have worked hard to make a comfortable life for my family, a life that was more financially secure than my parents provided for me. Not to say it was their fault because I'm not sure what circumstances they had encountered. Yet, at an early age, I was determined to take up that fight to be financially secure.

Little did I know that at some point in my life, I would not only be fighting to keep my family secure, but I would also be fighting for every breath that I managed to take. I am now facing the reality that I may have to live permanently with the battle scars I received fighting an unseen enemy that had invaded my body and was attempting to take whatever life I had left. The strength I developed to battle this enemy, which was officially called Covid-19, was three-fold in nature. Not only did I have to use my physical strength, which consisted of my antibodies, but also the antibodies that were injected into me. In addition, I relied on my spiritual strength and the spiritual strength of others at the most critical times.

I am what the scientific community calls a long hauler, a term that was not in my vocabulary prior to my experience. At this point, you may be asking the question how is my experience different than all the others? In response, I would have to say you will have to read my story to find out. I had the idea for writing about my experience when I started getting a lot of questions on social media about how I was coping with my illness. A lot of the questions dealt with my experience while I was on a ventilator in a coma. It was an experience that not many people live to talk about, and it is my quest to share with others the images, visions, and feelings that I experienced.

After several social media postings, I decided to preserve the events, my feelings, my thoughts, and how this experience has impacted my present life. With true conviction, I can now admit that through adversity we become better people. I hope that through my experience I have learned that diversity shapes character and I, as well as others, will see that I am now a different person. At the very least, I can say that I now look at life from a different perspective. Where I place value in my life has changed, and my family is now closer and more loving than ever.

In the following pages, I am asking you to take a journey with me. I'll do my best to bring you into my life so that you may experience my thoughts, my feelings, and the events leading up to this monumental event in our history known as the Covid-19 pandemic. In addition, I hope that you will experience, as best as words can possibly manage, the extent of my fight with the virus.

Then, the effects physical, emotional, and spiritual that I now deal with on a regular basis. I hope that after reading my story you will have a better outlook on the events that situation as a means to build our character. The choice is up to you. However, in this important historical juncture, we face we have the opportunity as a community, nation, and world to make the changes necessary for our children and grandchildren to have a better life.

Before we delve into my story, let me introduce myself and share with you a little about my early life. These early life events are important because they shaped my persistence and drive to succeed. My name is Larry Mondragon, and I have to say that my life has been good.

Before graduating from high school, I dropped out of school to marry my first wife. We were both young and I felt the need to provide for our growing family. While working to make ends meet as an independent contractor laying carpet and floor materials, I completed my General Equivalency Diploma. It wasn't long before I was providing for a family of three children: Sharon, Felisha, and Mario. As I reflect on that period of my life, I think it's safe to say that I married at a time when my wife and I were still kids.

Through the years, we grew up in our relationship and found out that the love we thought we had may have been hinged on infatuation rather than the true love needed to prolong our marriage. As a result, my first marriage dissolved.

Battling the Beast – Through the power of prayer

I was a carpet installer for about seventeen years, which was my means of providing for my family. Also, as a side job, I was a musician. Since I was in elementary school, I made a small amount of money in the evenings and weekends playing guitar and singing in various dance bands. Music became a passion for me and a means to learn about the entertainment industry. There was a part of me that hoped to make music a career, but the reality of providing stability for my family, outweighed the risk.

After my divorce, a career change was in order. The many years of being on my hands and knees installing carpet and floor coverings took a toll on my legs.

As a result, I took a chance on being a car salesman. I discovered that I had a knack for salesmanship and the opportunities for advancement were promising.

I met my second wife, Mary, and together added to our family three more children: Christina, Joshua, and Molly. Since I was making a decent income in sales, I decided to renew my passion for music. As a compromise, I combined the skills I learned in sales and the skills I learned in the entertainment industry to promote musical talent. Being a concert promoter, I brought to the Pueblo community several well-known acts for entertainment.

Working hard in my career allowed me to provide well for my family. I did well with my investments and I climbed myself into a comfortable income bracket.

I was finally in a position where I didn't have to worry about money problems as I believed my parents struggled with.

In late 2019, I partnered with John Secora, another concert promoter, to plan for a Spring Summer Jam. There was a lot of work planning for the event: finding the right musical talent that fits the demographic region, negotiating contracts and details with agents and managers, rental of a venue, advertising, stagehands, hotel bookings, food, and ticket sales, just a short list. We set a concert date for March 20th, 2020, the first day of spring. We were hoping that news of a possible pandemic would not affect the show.

It is here that my story begins. As you read through the pages, there are times I may reflect on an earlier date, realizing the information is pertinent to the overall story.

I hope that you will vicariously live the events through me, and in the end, you too may have a heightened appreciation for life. It is a fact that everyone on earth will someday face death, but how we face that time depends on our outlook on life. Will you be able to look back on your past years and genuinely admit that you fought the good life? I hope that after hearing my story you will reflect on your own life and possibly make the necessary changes to stand firm when life gives you lemons and celebrate when victories come your way.

Table of Contents

Dedication iii

Introduction iv

Chapter 1 1

Chapter 2 8

Chapter 3 17

Chapter 4 23

Chapter 5 28

Chapter 6 36

Chapter 7 43

Chapter 8 54

Chapter 9 63

Chapter 10 74

Chapter 11 87

1

The year started off with an eerie feeling as if something didn't seem right. The best way to describe the feeling is similar to when birds begin gathering in hordes, squawking in the trees as if warning others of an impending disaster. I knew our country had its share of domestic and political problems in 2019, but I felt hopeful that these problems would improve in 2020. It seemed like the news and social media platforms were at odds with each other. It was easy to wonder if their agenda was to divide the country.

Since this was an election year, I knew the political climate would be electrifying. Electing a new president was always a decisive decision for our political party system. Promises were made by the presidential candidates that surely would leave one to wonder if the promises were only political rhetoric. It was difficult to keep up with the ad campaigns coming from the democrats, the republicans, the conservatives, and the progressives.

In the midst of the political jabs, news broke out of a potentially deadly virus coming out of China. This was early January and the news was hardly earth-shattering, at least not yet. Rumors began circulating that the virus had originated from bats or had been manufactured in a Chinese lab experimenting with germ warfare. More importantly, it was also rumored that the news was another political scare to boost a certain political party. In the midst of all that was going on, the most important news was that our present president was in the process of being impeached.

My hometown of Pueblo, Colorado is a city that is big enough that everyone minds their own business, and yet small enough that we rarely make the national news. Natural disasters are almost non-existent, even the big snow storms have become less frequent with many believing it's due to global warming. We have the same problems as other cities with gun violence and what to do with our homeless population, but each day passes uneventfully. It was one of these normal mornings when I was on my way to work at the same job I had for 30 years. I am not complaining. I like my job. I work in financing at a reputable car dealership. It is my responsibility to help customers find a financing option that will help them buy an automobile. I was listening to the radio on my way to work when I heard the shocking news of a helicopter crash. My favorite basketball player Kobe Bryant and his daughter had been killed in a crash in California. What a tragedy for his family and all his fans. The news made me think of my own daughters and thankful they were safe.

I'm not the kind of person that thinks much about the news, but after Kobe Bryant's crash, I was drawn to the news around the world. Unfortunately, I was not prepared for the next story that hit the airwaves.

According to the World Health Organization, the concern over the virus in China had widened to the extent that a pandemic may be in the making. Of course, the news concerned me. Several worries passed through my mind.

What would life be like in the event that we were required to quarantine? What would be the protocol? I'm not one to panic, but I did not want to see my wife, kids, or grandkids catch the virus. According to the news, the government is downplaying the seriousness of the problem, which concerns me.

Much of the country, at least the southeastern and eastern coasts, is still dealing with the devastation of hurricane Dorian in 2019. Mass shootings were becoming more common in the news, and even small children in schools were not exempt from these tragedies. Scientists have been warning us about global warming for several years, but their pleas are becoming more desperate. For evidence, they have turned to the escalation of natural disasters.

Forest fires, floods, hurricanes, and tornados have all grown in frequency and intensity. I have to wonder if this is what the Bible eludes too in the end times. In Revelation 12:1-2, it says the end times will be like a woman giving birth to a child, suffering with the pains of childbirth. I have to wonder if these are all signs that we are living in the last days.

Our government seems so divided right now as the democratic-led House of Representatives impeached our president, knowing that the republican Senate will undoubtedly vote to acquit him. At the Republican Convention in Springfield, Illinois on June 16th, 1858, Abraham Lincoln said, "A house divided cannot stand." He was referring to the latest controversy of whether to own slaves or not, but the rift in our government still is similar. Our present governmental problem has seeped into the everyday life of our society. Republican and democratic issues have divided neighbors, friends, and even family members.

Our society is dealing with several problems in urban communities. The opoid crisis would be at the top of that list. Doctors and pharmaceutical companies are being indicted for their contribution to the addictive nature of pain killers. Our emergency medical response teams are being over-taxed by the increase in overdose calls. It makes a person have to wonder if the addiction is a cause of physical pain or an escape from some type of emotional pain.

It seems like many of our cities are dealing with their share of a growing homeless population. In my hometown, the homeless congregate near the river's edge, living in makeshift tents. During the day, it's common to find them panhandling in areas where the traffic is most congested, hoping that a passerby will stop and give some type of handout. When I witness this firsthand, I've often wondered if the surges in opiate addiction and homelessness are related. Each addict or homeless person has a story unique to their situation. Was it a failed marriage, a job that was terminated, or a streak of several bad luck circumstances, or could it be that our society has failed them. Then to add to the problems, many of those in these two categories are veterans. Men and women who have fought for our freedom and returned home with problems related to their service. As a government and society, we have failed these patriots in uniform by ignoring their problems and letting them down in the adjustment of returning home to a society that has become calloused to their reintegration back as contributing citizens.

In the summer of 2019, my wife, Mary, my daughter, Molly, and I took a vacation to Washington D.C, and New York City, cities that we had hoped to see in our lifetimes. The experience was amazing as we marveled at the many historical landmarks. Having an avid interest in history, I was amazed by the historical buildings in Washington. I was especially fascinated by the tour of the White House, causing me to feel like a child in a candy store.

While in New York City, we couldn't help but notice the large homeless population that was sleeping in the streets. It was sad to see that the homeless consisted of many young children, and a fair amount of them seemed to be under the influence of drug use. My family and I discussed the matter and wondered if the drugs had finally taken a toll on the parents, which resulted in the children moving out to sleep elsewhere.

The scene reminded me of some communities that were preparing for a zombie apocalypse, and if the sci-fi scenario would ever become reality, it would probably look similar to the homeless, drug-infested streets of New York City. Even though I enjoyed the trip, the reality that many of our historical cities also had a dark side was eye-opening.

Little did anyone know that an event in 2019 will

change everyone's lives around the world. History has revealed to us that certain notable events have been so horrific that it has affected our everyday lives. In the last century, our world was engaged in two wars. Certain events during that time shaped the present and our future. For example: during World War II several significant events were pivotal in our nation's history. The aerial attack at Pearl Harbor took us by surprise as the war came to our own borders and ushered in our declaration of war on Japan. Even President Roosevelt was accredited with saying, "This day will live on in infamy"

World War II, as with other wars, was vicious.
We as a nation were the first to drop an atomic bomb on one of our enemies. Some may argue that our response was excessive. We not only bombed Hiroshima on August 6, 1945, but three days later dropped another bomb on Nagasaki. 120, 000 Japanese citizens were estimated to be killed. Many historians believe the bombings brought the Japanese to the surrender table. Did the sacrifice of 120,000 Japanese stop the killing of hundreds of thousands of our own troops and allies? We will never know the true answer to that question, but we can only speculate.
Even to this day, many Japanese live with the effects of the radioactive exposure that has been handed down for generations.

Another life-changing historical event that is worthy to be mentioned is the morning of September 11, 2001. Terrorism on our soil became a real event. As with Pearl Harbor, our country was blindsided by an attack that caught us off guard. Many were watching the news as a commercial airline was hijacked and rammed into the side of one of the twin towers. At first viewing, many speculated the crash may have been an accident, but then shortly after the first attack, a second airplane crashed into the second tower.

Another airplane was also reported to have crashed into the Pentagon in Arlington, Virginia, and another crashed in Shanksville, Pennsylvania. It is documented that 2,977 people were killed that day; 2,763 were in the World Trade Center and the surrounding area, 189 were at the pentagon, and 44 were in Pennsylvania, along with 19 hijackers that committed murder-suicide. The terrorist attack had a changing effect on our daily lives, as well as changes to our national security.

Even to this day, we see many of those changes in the security protocols in our airports. Additional restricted fly zones have been added to our air space, and our air force is better prepared to handle such a situation if another one occurs.
It took a monumental event such as this to open up our eyes to the possibility that other terroristic threats are looming just around the corner.

There are numerous other events that have shaped our nation, and still others that have impacted our personal lives that may be more localized. Yet, it is apparent that world, national and local events, whether they are classified as good or bad, have the potential to affect our everyday lives.

2

In early 2020, it became clear that many of our health organizations were concerned the virus, Covid-19, is evolving into a pandemic. Several countries are reporting the virus outbreak, including the United States. However, our president is downplaying the virus as something similar to the flu.

He is saying that once the weather warms up the virus will disappear. Yet, the Centers for Disease Control is beginning to make preparations to protect the public. Responses such as; mask mandates, quarantines, anti-viral medications, and vaccines, became frequent conversation topics on our news outlets and talk shows.

Finally, in response to the national attention on the subject, President Trump appointed the Vice-President, Mike Pence, to a specialized committee to address the Covid-19 virus.

According to the newly appointed White House Task Force, the virus is known to attack the body's respiratory system. The symptoms associated with the illness included dry cough, runny nose, headache, fever, chills, and body aches. The medical community is encouraging people with symptoms to stay home and quarantine. However, if the conditions worsen then it is wise to contact a physician. Several news outlets are reporting a rise in patients being seen in the emergency rooms with breathing problems and testing positive for the virus. As a result, the intensive care units are filling at an alarming rate. In early February 2020, the first death associated with the virus was reported in Santa Clara County, California. It is now speculated that the virus had been around for several weeks prior to that time.

If Covid-19 is similar to the flu, then how much worse can it get? It is a known fact that the flu takes the lives of many each year, then why is the scientific community concerned about this new illness? These questions were passing through my mind as I'm sure many other Americans had similar thoughts. Then, the CDC announced that the virus could be as much as ten times more contagious than the flu, and if anyone caught the illness, they were more likely to die from complications.

Once again, the political division is apparent. One side is blaming the other for exaggerating the severity of the virus, while the other side saying not enough is being done to address the issue. I found myself in the center, wondering what side to believe. I wonder if it is an election year that only adds fuel to the fire. I'm sure that neither party wants to be on the losing side. My awareness of our political system has deepened. I am convinced that the strategies used to be re-elected do not necessarily mean the difference between right and wrong, but rather what can be done to secure the winning votes.

On Thursday, March 12, 2020, reality finally hit the sporting community. The National Basketball League Board of Governors halted all games until further notice.

According to the announcement, the NBA administration was concerned over possible positive test results of several Utah Jazz players. The Jazz was slated to play the Oklahoma City Thunder but concerns over the uncertainties of the virus and how it would affect the other players, coaches, and fans, warranted an abundance of caution under the circumstances.

Shortly after the NBA's announcement the governor of Colorado, Jared Polis, held a news conference detailing the impact of Covid-19 in Colorado. At this time there were 72 confirmed cases, which increased from 49 the day before. The governor also added that at least four of the cases were evidence of community spread from the Denver metro area. There were also eight people in the hospital and three of those were in critical condition.

Governor Polis emphasized in his announcement that it was only a matter of time before Colorado had its first fatality. To protect the public and forestall the virus, the governor issued some recommendations for mass gatherings.

Groups of over 250 people were discouraged unless each person practiced social distancing, which meant allowing a distance of six feet between individuals. Within days the governor's recommendation changed considerably. His recommendation changed from a recommendation to a mandate, prohibiting all gatherings of over 50 people. I'm sure that his decision was based on the severity and quick spread of the virus.

Soon after the governor's announcement, John Secora, my business partner, and I received word from the concert venue that our Spring Jam event slated for March 20th, will have to be canceled in order to comply with the state's mandate.

To reach the ticketholders of the cancellation, I turned to social media. In my post, I made sure to mention the event was canceled due to the pandemic and the mandate of restricting gatherings of no more than 50 people. Our Spring Jam concert was expected to bring in attendance far more than 50 people. I also emphasized that all tickets would be refunded at the box office where the tickets were sold. I made sure to mention in the post that we were disappointed in the cancellation, but the public's safety was more important to us. In addition, we made it clear that if all possible we would reschedule the event at a later date. Next, I notified our promotional sponsors of the cancellation and refunded any money that had already been paid for advertising.

Being a musician myself, it was easy to see how the cancellation of our Spring Jam concert would affect the musicians and performers in our particular community. I then begin wondering how this virus, along with the social restrictions, would affect musicians all across our country as well as other countries across the globe.

I was disappointed that our small show affected jobs for over fifty people. The pandemic was beginning to take an effect on the entertainment industry in my own community, and I could only imagine the effect it is having on not only the entertainment industry across our country but also the sports teams. The National Basketball Association had already responded by canceling their upcoming games, but the other sports teams are yet to be affected. If the course of the virus continues to spread in severity and transmission, the workforce, in general, has the potential of being hit hard. Also, social gatherings at various venues from bars to family favorites; such as water parks, zoos, amusement parks, and museums, may have to close until the virus is under control. I could only imagine how this would affect the labor force, as well as the mental health of the people in quarantine. More importantly, this pandemic has the potential of destroying our world economy.

Today is March 16, 2020; and the inevitable has just happened. The Governor of Colorado has just announced the closure of all bars and restaurants in the state. In addition, he instituted a mask mandate, requiring mask-wearing in all public places along with social distancing between individuals at least six feet apart.

He emphasized these measures are required to curb the spread of the disease. The pandemic has introduced two new concepts into our daily life: mask mandates and social distancing. The medical community has become more vocal in stressing the importance of frequent hand washing and sanitizing areas that we touch regularly.

There is a lot of buzz on social media about how this will affect everyone's lives. As a result, people are starting to panic. This is evident by the rush at the grocery stores to buy essential items.

Toilet tissue, paper towels, hand sanitizers, and disinfectant sprays, are becoming difficult to find. The stores were having a hard time stocking these items, and in some cases had to limit the amount a person could buy.

I recall when I was a young boy my father worked at the local steel mill. It was early in the 1960s when the steel mill workforce went on strike, leaving my dad without work for several months. As a result, my family had to learn how to ration the available food. My parents had to make do with feeding a family of seven: four sons and one daughter. I remember my parents taking the whole family to work in the farmer's fields, and my parents were paid a few dollars per day for their work. Several of my siblings and I were too young to work very long at wrapping celery, picking chili and tomatoes, topping onions, and so forth, but we entertained ourselves playing in the rows of vegetables.

Since my father's income was meager, our family qualified for government commodities, which consisted of cheese, butter, powdered milk, beans, rice, potatoes, flour, sugar, and various canned goods. These items were selected because of their long shelf life or with minimal refrigeration. With this memory in mind, I decided to purchase similar items, along with toiletries and bottled water. This pandemic was all new to me and I felt the necessity to protect my family and make sure that we had the essential foods and supplies to endure a long haul if necessary.

Another thought that came to mind was whether I was prepared to protect my family in case some looters decided to take what I had in storage, which included supplies and anything of value. I have never been a person wanting to keep guns in my house, much less carry a firearm. At an early time, I reluctantly owned several rifles that I used for elk and deer hunting. The hunting party usually consisted of a few friends and me, although I enjoyed the camaraderie more than the killing of defenseless animals. After the hunting activity lost its appeal and I didn't care for the taste of the meat, I disposed of the guns. However, with the current state of things and the potential for social unrest, I am rethinking the possibility of purchasing firearms again.

I told myself a long time ago that if I ever consider purchasing a firearm for protection, then I need to have the courage to pull the trigger if I need to protect myself or my family from an intruder or a looter. After much thought over the matter and realizing the potential for civil unrest if the pandemic escalates out of control, my family is the most important part of my life and as a husband and a father, I need to protect them no matter what the cost. Do I have the courage to pull the trigger, which is different than hunting elk or deer, if human life is at risk? That question remains to be tested if the situation arises. Nevertheless, I feel I am prepared to handle such a situation, but hope that the opportunity to test such a scenario will never surface.

I went to the local Walmart to buy a few items and noticed the place was packed with more shoppers than usual.

Many of the shopper's carts were filled with meats, bottled water, beer, toilet paper, and paper towels, enough to stock up for months. It seemed to me like the scene was a little hectic as if shoppers were stocking up out of fear and panic. I was surprised that some of the shelves were emptying fast, and others required being restocked. I had already stocked up on some essentials, but thankfully, I have a brother-in-law that works at a whole foods warehouse. Knowing the situation, I was able to give him a list of grocery essentials, which he was able to fill.

The news media announced that nationwide there is a toilet paper shortage. If the stores have toilet tissue in stock, they are limiting the amount any one person can buy. Some people are waiting in line for hours to get their share, and arguments between shoppers are becoming plentiful. It's a little surreal to witness this firsthand. It reminds me of a hint of what our society will be like when the apocalypse arrives. People are posting on social media what stores have toilet paper, but within minutes the stock is gone. Toilet paper is becoming rare to find and in some cases when found on the internet stores, the price is elevated tenfold. Also, the news media is blaming the shortage on the vast amount of shoppers that buy more than needed for hoarding or for reselling at a higher price. Could toilet paper be the new currency for the future? That's a thought worth considering.

Many states are reporting a rise in hospitalizations due to the virus spreading. It has become impossible for our President to ignore the facts and the science behind the disease's high rate of transmission and its severity.

In response, President Trump issued a national emergency, which will help to free up much-needed funds for the hard-hit areas. However, even after the CDC's recommendation to wear a mask while in public and practice social distancing, the President refuses to do either. Information from the news outlets seems to suggest he is still blaming the democrats for misinformation and exaggerating the severity of the pandemic.

Since President Trump has a large republican following, his actions have created a problem for the general public. Since he is refusing to follow the CDC's mask-wearing guidelines and social distancing, his followers feel they could do the same.

Conflicts and violent outbursts are increasing as store owners and restaurants are trying to abide by the state's mandate of mask-wearing, but clashing with individuals that refuse to abide by the mandate. It seems apparent that many of the people bucking the mask mandate are republicans and loyal followers of President Trump. The problem that it creates on a larger scale is the division in our political system only grows wider.

3

As I reflect on the year, the one good thing that happened was the beginning of my weight loss journey. With the pandemic spreading throughout the country, I decided it was time to get healthier. I was determined to improve my immune system to stave off the virus. As part of my routine, along with better eating habits, I would start the morning with a protein shake for breakfast, then spend an hour walking at a brisk pace on the treadmill. My diet consisted of minimizing my carbohydrate intake, which I knew from past experiences some weight loss would occur. I have lost forty pounds in the past four months of this regiment. Since the virus is spreading, I'm sure I am not alone in trying to improve my health to prevent the possible outcome of catching the disease. Whether my attempt will be successful remains to be determined.

The owners of the dealership I work at called a special meeting today. Governor Polis has just issued a stay-at-home order. The dealership owners called the meeting to inform their employees that to comply with the governor's mandate, and everyone would be laid off until further notice. In addition, they encouraged everyone to apply for unemployment benefits.

According to the governor's mandate, only essential businesses were allowed to remain open. He also advised businesses, if possible, to have their employees work from home. Yet, there is widespread confusion about what businesses are considered essential. Since I am now laid off, I guess the automotive industry was not considered essential. What baffles me, and I'm sure others had the same thoughts, is what makes places like the big chain stores and the banks essential. I can see the necessity of grocery stores and gas stations, but the definition of what makes a business essential seems to be a bit ambiguous.

Mary, my wife, heard that she would be able to continue working. Since she works at a bank, she is considered an essential worker. However, several precautions were instituted: the lobby inside the bank was closed to patrons, and only the drive-thru was open for business. Also, online banking was recommended to limit contact with others that may be infected or carriers of the virus.

After being told I was laid off from the car dealership, I returned home to begin applying for unemployment benefits. Since this was the first time I've ever applied for benefits, the process was all new to me.

Fortunately, within three days, I was called back to work. Yet, like the bank my wife worked at, several precautions were set in place. After Governor Polis's stay-at-home order and the closing of essential businesses, a variety of business owners had questioned the term of essential businesses. Our car dealership was able to compromise by minimizing contact with its customers. For example, an appointment was required when a customer was interested in purchasing a particular car. If a potential buyer wanted to take a vehicle on a test drive, he or she did it alone without a salesman present. In addition, all the paperwork and negotiations were done on the phone or the Internet. If a sale is made, the automobile was thoroughly sanitized and delivered to its new owner utilizing mask-wearing and social distancing.

The car dealership only asked a few employees to return to work, which was considered a skeleton crew. Since I was trained in finance, I was one of the fortunate to be included in this minimal crew. The other members included the owner's immediate family and managers with experience negotiating and preparing the paperwork for potential buyers. Also, a few employees returned that had experience with Internet negotiations, which was necessary to maintain social distancing and minimize contact between the salesperson and the car buyers.

This new way of selling cars was strange, to say the least, in a business that in the past had been dependent on close interaction between the salesperson and the potential buyers. Not only did the dealership institute very strict guidelines and protocols for operations, but the health department stepped in to add some of its own. The dealership owners also emphasized that it was important and necessary for all of its employees to strictly follow these guidelines and protocols for the business to remain open.

Since we were considered essential workers and the state was in lockdown, we were required to carry a letter, provided by the dealership, with us at all times stating so. If we were pulled over by authorities and did not have the letter in our possession, we could be ticketed for violating the stay-at-home order. I understood the need for rules at this time, but I felt skeptical about how such an order could be enforced. I wondered if the authorities had the manpower to police everyone out on the streets that didn't have a document.

Working with a deserted showroom void of customers and only the barebones of employees was not only different but also eerie. Since I am now working in an environment that follows all the strict guidelines and protocols, I may be biased, but I have to wonder how other large stores stay open with little restrictions on the number of patrons within their doors. How is it that these stores could allow numerous shoppers while our dealership, which usually has about 30 to 40 customers and employees, was required to minimize any contact with our customers and operate only with a skeleton crew?

This virus is not only taking a toll on car dealerships, but bars, restaurants, barbershops, and hair salons are all pondering whether they will be able to open after a sense of normalcy returns. I can see how it could be dangerous for bars to remain open. After a few drinks, a person's ability to understand the necessity for mask-wearing and social distancing is greatly reduced. However, these businesses will be hard hit by the closings, even if the closings were short-lived. Many of these businesses struggle in the best of times, but losing their patrons for a significant period will be devastating.

I never thought in my wildest dreams that a fashion trend would emerge over mask-wearing. From online retailers to department stores, a person can order and buy various types and styles of masks. As I see others in public or notice the onslaught of online advertisements, face coverings can be found with business logos, sports teams, and various colors and sizes ranging from toddlers to adults. I've also noticed that many people have coordinated the color and style of their masks with the clothes they picked out for the day.

Even though numerous states are under a mask mandate, some individuals still refuse to wear one in public. These individuals usually claim it is their right as a citizen of the United States to decide whether they want to wear one or not. This reason is concerning to me. Mask-wearing should only be a right as an American if it does not affect the health of self or others. It is obvious that wearing a face covering will minimize the spread of the virus by protecting the mask wearer and others they may come in contact with.

As I browsed through social media, I noticed the rise of videos taken of customers in stores that refused to wear masks. Many of the videos included heated arguments to all-out brawls. The store employees usually tried to enforce the mask mandate but ran into resistance from those who felt as if their rights were being violated. Sometimes the arguments and fights were between customers on both sides of the issue.

A new celebrity called "Karen" has emerged from

these types of videos. "Karen" is a fictitious person, a name associated with a chronic complainer who is known to be vocal on social media. Usually, this person is known to make some type of public scene as they protest some precautions associated with the pandemic. Also, this person is often a female, but when a male displays such behavior, he is called a "Ken."

Since the pandemic is crippling our economy, trickling down to individual families, our nation's lawmakers reacted by passing the Coronavirus Aid Relief and Economic Security Act, informally called the Cares Act, on March 27, 2020. The 2.2 trillion economic stimulus bill was intended as a lifeline to many families struggling to pay rent and buy groceries. The legislation sent direct payments of $1,200.00 to individuals making less than $75,000.00 per year and married couples making $150,000.00 or less. It also included an additional $700.00 for dependent children living in the household that were seventeen years of age or younger. These direct payments were given above and beyond any income or unemployment benefits anyone was receiving.

With hospitals operating near their maximum levels and the death toll from this virus nearing 100,000 people, the CDC began working with drug companies to find effective drug treatments. Two possible treatments were considered: Hydroxychloroquine and the experimental drug, Remdesivir. The first had been a common drug used to prevent and treat malaria.

4

We just sold our Pueblo West home of eighteen years and decided to find a home in the Pueblo City limits. The house in Pueblo West became too big to maintain since most of our children had grown up and moved out to live independently. Our new home in Pueblo was a tad smaller, but the yard needed some renovations for our liking. Our daughter, Molly, had several dogs that enjoyed playing out in the yard but ran into some problems with the sticker weeds that had overrun our lawn. After a while out in the yard, the dogs attracted a considerable amount of stickers to their fur coats, causing discomfort to the pets. Since my daughter spent a fair amount of time removing the stickers and I had time at home because of the stay-at-home orders, I decided to renovate the lawn. The process began with removing all the old lawn and replacing it with sod.

Since I had been handy with home projects, I took on the fun challenge of transforming the backyard. It was also an opportunity to put our stamp on our new home. Before beginning the process, I was surprised to find the two major home project stores were filled with patrons. With the lockdown in place, I guess my idea of utilizing the time to remodel was also on the minds of others.

After renting a sod cutter, the work began. I learned quickly that this project was not going to be as easy as I had imagined. I guess I could blame it on my age or my lack of this type of physical exercise. I soon discovered the sod-cutting machine's vibrating action as it cut and rolled the grass was difficult to handle. In addition, after the sod was cut in rolls, it had to be loaded in the back of a truck. The weed-infested sod rolls took up four truckloads to deliver to the dump. Needless to say, the first part of the yard renovation consisted of a considerable amount of physical exercise that pushed my limits of physical strength.

After clearing out the weed-infested sod, the backyard was ready for its renovation. I had envisioned the result, but in order to reach that goal, I had to plan each phase at a time. The first component to be installed was our hot tub. This was an item that was brought over from our previous home. Realizing I needed professional expertise for this phase, I hired a concrete installer and an electrician.
Within a week, the hot tub was installed, and this renovation phase was complete.

Since the house came with a large back deck, the next phase consisted of installing a pergola to the far end of our yard. To add to this feature, this phase also consisted of installing a flagstone walkway from the deck to the pergola. To eliminate some physical labor, I ordered the pergola online. In addition to the pergola, I also ordered some outdoor furniture and a propane fire pit table. The work of installing the flagstone walkway turned out to be quite strenuous. A trench had to be dug from the deck to the pergola, about eight inches deep, as a bed for the flagstone.

Next on my list was to level the ground with crushed granite and sand. I also poured concrete for the pergola's frame. After completing these tasks, it was time to pick out the type of flagstone to complete the walkway. I estimated that six tons of flagstones would be required to complete the job.

I underestimated the difficult work it would take to lay the flagstone. Not only was the work back-breaking, because of the weight of each flagstone, but I also had to battle with the intense summer heat. It was common for the temperature to be in the 90's or 100's. Even though this phase of the backyard renovation was labor intensive, I realized I had extra time to work on the project. The stay-at-home mandate of the pandemic had created the perfect opportunity to complete at-home work projects for many people. Since the renovation kept me at home, I was able to stay safe from those that may have been infected. I did have to patronize some stores when I purchased supplies, but I was careful to wear a mask, keep my distance, and frequently use hand sanitizer.

Even though the work was difficult, I'm thankful I committed to a diet and exercise program. Losing more than sixty pounds and exercising regularly helped my stamina and motivation to complete what I started.

After completing the pergola, the flagstone pathway and leveling out the yard, I took some time to gaze around the yard and admire the results. However, the yard seemed incomplete. There was still a large section that seemed to have no purpose. It was then that my daughter, Molly, suggested, "Dad, why don't you build an in-ground swimming pool."

Since Molly is my youngest, she didn't have the opportunity to enjoy the swimming pool we had at a previous house we owned as her older siblings were able to. She was born after we sold that house and only heard about the swimming pool from family stories. Since she enjoyed entertaining her friends and helped out around the house without complaint, I decided to heed her request.

As a father, I want my children to get the most out of life, and whenever possible, I want to provide things I could not have when I was a child. Since my work provided a secure financial future, I can now enjoy some reasonable materialistic purchases. With this in mind, I decided to take on the challenge of building the pool myself. I knew I would need to hire contractors to do the things I could not do or areas where a licensed professional was required.

After careful consideration, I searched the Internet for do-it-yourself pool kits. The inventory was extensive, but after considering the size of the area in my backyard, I settled on ordering a sixteen-foot by thirty-two-foot pool kit from an online warehouse. The pool kit came with a liner, ladders, a heater, filters, and an automatic pool cover. After I clicked the purchase button, I had second thoughts. Could this project be too big for me to handle? Yet, I thrived on challenges, and the lockdown gave me the time to tackle this project, a time I otherwise would not have had.

The pool kit was expected to arrive in six to eight

weeks, which gave me time to do the prep work. I began by hiring an excavator to dig the hole in the backyard. When my wife, Mary, saw the hole being dug, she thought I was crazy for taking on such a project.

For the digging equipment to enter the back yard, I had to knock down a cinderblock wall. With the right digging equipment being used, it didn't take long for the hole to be dug. Now it was my responsibility to level off the areas and shape the area that would hold the deep end. To add myself to this process, I rented a laser level to make sure the kit would be at ground level and even all around its sides. Next, I had to purchase and install about two inches of road base, which is crushed gravel, to form a hard surface. This had to be compacted and leveled. The road base is used to prevent the side panels of the kit from drooping and losing their level. Finally, in mid-July, the pool kit arrived. I suspected I would have the project finished and ready for use by the end of August.

You may be wondering how my yard project is relevant to my story. It's important because it's an integral part of the events leading up to my illness. The backyard project within itself did not cause my illness, but I believe, as you read further, that it contributed greatly to the illness's severity. I wonder if I took on too much physical labor that somehow affected my body's ability to ward off the virus.

5

The next morning, on the 14th of September, I woke up with severe body aches and flu-like symptoms. I knew it would be difficult to work with these symptoms, so I called my employer to let her know I wasn't feeling well and would not be coming to work. She was sympathetic and seemed genuinely concerned for my health. However, she advised me that the protocol for possible exposure to Covid required that I have a negative test before returning to work. I didn't even think there was a possibility I had contracted the virus. I thought my symptoms were due to the common cold or flu. I made several phone calls to find Covid testing sites, but I had difficulty finding sites that administered the rapid tests. If I was tested at one of the regular sites, the test results could take anywhere from thirty-six to forty-eight hours. I preferred the rapid test so that I could test negative and return to work at the earliest time possible.

By late afternoon, my condition had worsened. Not only did I have severe body aches, but I developed a dry cough and fatigue. After several phone calls, I found an Urgent Care facility that would be able to do a rapid test that same day. I waited for Mary, my wife, to get off work, and we left for me to get tested at Urgent Care. I recall being extremely nervous as we waited in the waiting room for the results. I had heard the horror stories of people catching the virus, ending up in critical care, and eventually needing a ventilator to breathe. I could not imagine myself in a similar situation in my wildest dreams. The waiting for my results seemed to pass like an eternity.

Finally, a nurse entered the room to give me the news I dreaded to hear; I had tested positive for Covid-19. Being concerned for Mary's well-being, we decided for her also to get tested. Even though she hadn't complained of any symptoms, we had been in close contact. After waiting again, we were told that she also tested positive. I do not panic easily, but it was hard to accept the devastating news. Immediately, we thought of our daughter, Molly. We called her at her work at a local fast-food restaurant. Knowing the situation and the dire need to get tested, she left work and arrived at Urgent Care for the test. She also hadn't experienced any known symptoms but had been in close contact with Mary and me. For the third time, I had to deal with the devastating news that my daughter also tested positive. In a matter of a short time, my world seemed to have turned upside down.

Since all three of us tested positive for the virus, we were required to quarantine for fourteen days. I was determined that we would get through this illness as quickly as possible. We were well prepared with several types of cold and flu medications and Tylenol for fever and body aches. Several family members and friends provided food at our doorstep, which was greatly appreciated.

The day after we were tested, I started to feel better, while on the other hand, Mary and Molly began to feel miserable.

I encouraged them to get up, move around, and eat some meals, but unfortunately, they preferred to stay in bed and sleep.

Since I was feeling better, I decided to get back to work on my backyard project. Things were going well until Thursday, the 17th of September. By this time, Mary and Molly seemed to be improving. I was in the process of carrying bags filled with sand out of the empty swimming pool when I noticed a shift in my health. My breathing became labored, making it difficult to breathe properly. My energy level crashed as I struggled to lift each sandbag. My first thought was that I wanted to sleep. It was evident that my illness had taken a turn for the worse. I was a bit confused and concerned about these new symptoms. I didn't feel any body aches or any cold-like symptoms. I had thought I had put the virus behind me, and now I was questioning whether my symptoms were due to a new illness or had I actually recovered from Covid.

Deciding to give in to the way I felt, I resigned to resting in bed. As I did with Mary and Molly, they encouraged me to get up, move around, eat some meals, and drink plenty of fluids. As I recall, I don't remember losing my sense of smell, which was a noted symptom of the virus, but the loss of taste, another symptom, was somewhat diminished. I also remember the liquids I drank seemed to have a strange metallic aftertaste.

My memory of events seemed like a blur for the next few days. I know for certain that I spent a considerable amount of time in bed, sleeping most of the time. On the 20th of September, my birthday, I vaguely remember Mary bringing me a club sandwich and a slice of my favorite dessert, cherry pie. I wasn't feeling well enough to take a bite of it either.

I regularly checked my oxygen level when I was awake, which usually dropped to eighty percent. This concerned me, knowing it was affecting my breathing or capability of doing so. I borrowed a portable oxygen concentrator from a friend to address the matter. In order to maintain an acceptable oxygen level, I was taking in three to four liters of oxygen per day.

On the morning of Monday, the 21st of September, I was concerned that my symptoms were severe enough that I felt as if my body was shutting down. I shared this with Mary, and knowing my situation was dire, she told me to get up because she was driving me to the emergency room.

When we arrived at the ER, Mary wasn't allowed to go in with me because of Covid protocols. Upon arriving, I advised the nurse on duty that I was not feeling well and had tested positive for the virus the week prior. She instructed me to wait outside until someone was available to come out and get me. I recall waiting outside, leaning against a pole, and wondering if I would pass out before help arrived. The waiting seemed like an eternity. Finally, a hospital worker arrived with a wheelchair to assist me.

Once back inside the hospital, I was taken straight to

the emergency room. The first thing the emergency room nurses did was take my vitals. When my blood oxygen level was checked, they told me it was in the 40s, which is dangerously low. In response, I was immediately given supplemental oxygen. I was told by one of the nurses that I came in for medical attention at the nick of time, and if I had waited longer, I probably wouldn't have made it.

I was told by a nurse that I was going to be admitted to the hospital and taken into the Intensive Care Unit. I knew I was ill, but I had underestimated its severity. Upon being set up in the ICU room, a nurse set up an IV in my arm, continued with my supplemental oxygen and checked my vitals regularly. I then called Mary to let her know the latest developments. I explained to her that according to hospital Covid protocols, visitors were not allowed to visit patients. Of course, this would make it difficult for her and me.

After the conversation with my wife, I felt the gravity of the situation settling in. I was not quite sure what to expect from this virus. Fear became my companion as I realized I would need to fight this illness without my wife by my side in a place that was foreign to me. I recall only a few times staying in a hospital but never in an I.C. unit. The closest I've come to a major surgery was a double knee replacement, which I spent several nights each time in a regular hospital room.

I was also told by a nurse that the virus had settled in my lungs. This would explain why I was having trouble with my breathing and needed supplemental oxygen. If I had not been on supplemental oxygen, my oxygen level would drop significantly.

Considering the circumstances, I passed a fairly comfortable first night, and it seemed as if my condition was improving. After some tests were taken, I discovered that I had developed Covid pneumonia, which meant liquid was building up in my lungs. As a response, the doctors treating me decided to try a new FDA-approved drug that showed some positive response to the virus called Remdesiver. I was also prescribed a second treatment, which was only used for severe Covid patients, called convalescent plasma. This procedure was used to implant antibodies in the body to help battle the virus. The plasma was taken from recovered Covid patients. According to what I was told, recovering patients had developed these antibodies to combat the virus, and in my case, my body had insufficient antibodies to battle the virus. As a result, it was believed the plasma antibodies would help build my immune system to fight Covid-19.

Even though I was being told by the hospital staff that I was a sick man, I actually didn't feel that bad. My appetite was satisfactory, and my sense of smell and taste didn't seem to be a problem. These senses were only diminished a few days before being admitted to the hospital. I remember having a problem with shortness of breath and a cough, which was more severe when lying on my back. As a result, the nurses had me lying on my stomach at night, advising me this would help with my lungs. Yet, this position was uncomfortable, and many times throughout the night, I would wake with coughing spells. I was given a cough medicine to combat the coughing.

To pass my time, I watched a lot of news on television, from CNN to Fox. The virus dominated the news as each channel covered the number of people in hospitals and the number of deaths from the pandemic. The news portrayed a grim outlook for the future until scientists discovered vaccinations and then administered shots in people's arms. Sara, the head nurse, came into my room one day and offered me some advice. She emphasized that it may not be good for me psychologically to be watching so much news about the pandemic and suggested I watch something different to take my mind off the virus.

Before taking Sara's advice, I remember watching a CNN segment where Chris Cuomo talked about having Covid and dealing with it at home. He mentioned the symptoms being worse at night as his fever climbed. He referred to this time as when the beast would come out.
I wasn't quite sure what he meant by this, but I wondered if it was something that was personal to him.

Throughout my ordeal, I didn't battle with fever, which maybe was one of the reasons the virus settled in my lungs. I've heard that fever is one of the symptoms that means your body is battling with the virus in your body. Maybe my body didn't have the antibodies necessary to fight the infection.

It's been five days since I was admitted into the ICU. I'm finding that each day my breathing becomes more difficult. I am now required to lie down on my stomach for at least nine hours a day. This position is uncomfortable, especially when I need supplemental oxygen and a bi-pap machine to help with my breathing.

6

The seriousness of my illness is finally sinking in, making me wonder if my life could be on the line. Could this be how I face the end as I gasp for every breath I take? In my whole life, I was never tempted to take up the habit of smoking, knowing that doing so could potentially damage my lungs.

Yet, a virus, unknown by the scientific community only recently, has managed to attack my lungs like smoking could not. It's ironic to imagine that I did everything I could to protect my lungs, yet, I was attacked by something I could not see.

I'm concerned that I am losing my appetite; food just doesn't seem appealing. My guess is that this is another indication that my illness is getting worse. To rid my lungs of the mounting fluid buildup, the doctors prescribed the diuretic, Lasix. Being on a diuretic, I was frequently up and down to urinate. The movement caused severe coughing attacks, depleting what little strength was left in my body. At times like this, I was convinced the doctors, nurses, and support staff were doing everything possible to save my life. However, at times like this, I also battled with loneliness, wishing that Mary, my wife, could be by my side. I craved her comforting touch more than the bare essentials of food and water.

The suspicion that my health was deteriorating

became evident when I received a visit from an ICU physician. I was informed that I was a very sick man, and as I expected, he and his staff have been doing everything they could to help me. Yet, some important decisions may be forthcoming. If their current mode of treatment, which included the oxygen treatment, the diuretic, steroids, IV fluids, breathing treatments, and Covid experimental medications, did not work, then putting me in an induced coma and on a ventilator may be the next option. He emphasized I needed to be patient to see if the current treatment would work. Yet, I wondered why he mentioned the ventilator if it was not a plan he was considering.

After the doctor left, I was alone to my thoughts. I had worked my whole life to give my family the best I could offer.

Although, now that I am examining what is really important in my life, I realized it was not the material things that meant the most to me. I have to admit that I regret that I could have spent less time at work and more time at home with my family. Time was a priceless gift that did not require a price tag. I was determined to stay strong for Mary, Molly, and the rest of my family. It will be difficult, but I am also determined to hide my discouragement when I have conversations with them on the phone. This is the only contact I have with them, and I want them to know that I am handling this predicament with strength and dignity even though I am hiding the fear of the unknown.

Even though I am not quite yet fighting for my life,

my situation has the potential to change from day to day. I believe the ICU doctor was preparing me for such a turn in my condition. With this in mind, it's only natural for me to reflect on the possibility of the worst-case scenario. I am only a few years from considering retirement, and the thought of not being able to fulfill my retirement dreams with Mary is disheartening. We had hoped to spend our time traveling and growing old together. Will that dream now be only a dream?

All these thoughts pass through my mind as I lie in my bed. Will my future be cut short because of an unseen virus?

I'm trying my best to be positive, but I think it may be necessary to prepare my family for the possibility I won't be coming home. I knew that at some time in my life, I would be facing death, but I didn't think I would do so at such an early age. Since I had taken out a hefty insurance policy many years ago, I knew Mary would be financially secure if anything happened to me.

I've often wondered if I would be afraid when I knew that death was knocking at my door, and I think now I can honestly say that it's not death I fear but the uncertainty of what lies beyond. I also wondered if I have the energy or the strength to continue fighting the virus if my condition deteriorates. Nevertheless, this may not be my decision to make. At some point, I need to put my life and the expertise of my caregivers in God's hands and rest assured that whatever happens will be God's will.

On September 30, 2020, I received a visit from a person from palliative care. At the time, I was unsure what palliative care meant, but I learned their job was to work in conjunction with my doctors and nurses to make difficult decisions if and when the time arises. This may include decisions when a person is facing death, considering a nursing home, or needing hospice care services.

The woman was very direct as she asked questions pertaining to a living will, whether I wanted to be resuscitated if my treatment failed, and whether or not I wanted to be put on life support.

She also asked if I was prepared if I needed to be transferred to a nursing home facility. I emphasized that I wanted the hospital to do whatever was necessary to keep me alive. As I thought about my answer, I added that if I were in that bad shape, I would leave those decisions to my wife.

When the person left, I was left with a host of questions and feelings that I needed to sort out. "

Was my condition such that I could be facing death, and if so, could this hospital room be the last room I see? Not being able to see my wife and family in person was discouraging. Would the doctors and nurses be the last people my eyes will remember? When the time comes, will the pain be intolerable and too much for me to bear?"

"Is this how I imagined my life would end? What kind of legacy will I be remembered by? Will the people who knew me to say I was a good person? Did I do everything I could to show my wife and family that I deeply love them?"

All these questions and feelings passed quickly through my mind like a wind had entered the room through an opened window and exited as quickly as it had come.

As I keep reminding myself, I need to remain strong for my wife and family because if they see me strong, they, too, will try to face whatever comes with strength for my sake.

Over the next couple of days, my condition didn't seem to improve. I remember my chest feeling like it was on fire. I now understand what Chris Cuomo from CNN meant when he said that the beast came out at night. He was referring to his bout with the virus. My chest was so congested that my lungs were producing a strange wheezing sound. It reminded me of the sound a possessed person made in a horror movie. It made me wonder how much damage was being done to my lungs and whether the damage would be permanent.

On the morning of October 2, a nurse entered my room to let me know the doctor had left orders to install a catheter in me. I was a bit surprised but wondered if it had to do with getting up and down to use the bathroom, which resulted in coughing attacks. The catheter would allow me to keep resting on my stomach and, hopefully, allow my lungs to heal.

The next morning is a day I'll remember for the rest of my life. The day was October 3, 2020. Early that morning, I received a visit from the head doctor dealing with my care along with the palliative care person.

The doctor approached my bed and said, "Mr. Mondragon, you are very ill, and we are concerned that you are not going to make it. We can give you medication to keep you comfortable, but we estimate that you could pass in the next few days. We can try putting you on a ventilator, but we don't feel very optimistic it will work. If you want us to put you on a ventilator, then we need your permission to do so. We need your answer quickly because your oxygen level keeps dropping dangerously low, and we don't know how long your heart can manage the oxygen deprivation."

I responded, "I would like to try the ventilator, but I want to discuss it with my wife. How long do I have to make the decision?"

"About ten minutes," the doctor instructed. "We have everything in the hall and ready to go."

I now had to make a very difficult phone call to my wife. I know that everyone will someday face death, but I'm sure everyone hopes that time will come after a full life. It's sad when that time is cut short by an accident or an incurable illness. Even though I was facing the unknown, with the doctor giving me a less than fifty-fifty chance of survival on a ventilator, I still wanted to believe that I still had many years to live. With this in mind, I called my wife. I explained to her that I was going to be placed in a medically induced coma along with a ventilator to help me breathe. I added that this was my best chance of surviving. I told her that I loved her and to tell the kids that I loved them too. I asked her to get our finances in order, hope for the best, and prepare for the worst. I then said "goodbye," but she refused to say it back, but rather she said, "I'll see you later." I then ended the conversation with, "I'll see you later."

After the phone call, I permitted my caregivers to put me on a ventilator. The nurses and doctors worked fast, and before I knew it, I was out.

7

The following chapters are dreams and visions that I recall from the time I was in a medically induced coma. Some of what I remember may seem bizarre and may not make much sense, while others you may be able to understand the significance. I have included this section because I have had many questions from friends and acquaintances concerning what I remember while I was in a coma. I have tried my best to explain the dreams and what I call visions in as much detail as possible.

There are many people who believe that dreams or visions have a spiritual connection, while others believe they are only fragments of images that are floating around in our subconscious mind. A religious person may interpret their dreams and visions as a means for God to communicate in some enigmatic way. As an example, a person may have a dream that a loved one is in danger and is in need of saving. After waking, the person discovers the information was true and works with the authorities to rescue their loved one. Is this divine intervention or coincidence?

The study of dreams and visions, especially when a person experiences a near-death event, is popular in the Christian community.

What happens to a person's spirit at the time when death is imminent? There are numerous documented accounts of near-death events that speak of a bright light and an encounter with a spiritual being that is present to guide the person on their way into the light. Obviously, these events result in the person being advised that they need to return to earth. As you read through my dreams and visions, you may read some examples of what could be divine intervention, while others may just be passing thoughts or memories floating through my unconscious mind. I have not interpreted which may be spiritual and which could be just independent pieces of memories floating through my unconscious. I believe each person may interpret them according to their own beliefs or at least enjoy their reading as a glimpse into the mind of an unconscious person in a medically induced coma.

While in the coma, the first thing I remember was being in a beautiful field.

I believe this field may have been an alfalfa field. A slight breeze blew the alfalfa stalks gently back and forth as if welcoming my presence. The sun was shining at its fullest, and I noticed a few trees in the distance. Also, shadows of people appeared around me. I could make out the outline of their bodies, but their faces were a blur.

It was then that I realized these shadows were relatives of mine that had passed away. Even though I could not clearly see their faces, I knew from their body shapes that my mother and father were among them. Next to my parents were aunts, uncles, and a host of other relatives.

I noticed the man and woman next to my mother

were my grandparents. I knew this because I remember my grandfather as tall and thin with a large nose that was distinctive of our Native American heritage. I recall my grandmother being short and stocky.

The scene was surreal to me. I felt at peace, and I was amazed by its beauty. I peered around and saw rows and rows of flowers that reminded me of lilacs.

There were also mixed in among the flowers, what I believe were dandelions. The field reminded me of the scene from the Wizard of Oz when Dorothy, the Tin Man, the Scarecrow, the Lion, and Toto passed through the poppy field on their way to the Emerald City.

Not only did I have an overwhelming sense of peace, but I also felt as if my parents were there to welcome and comfort me on whatever journey awaited me. I then noticed a girl emerge from a distance walking in my direction. When she was a short distance away, I could see her face clearly, unlike the others, which seemed to be in a blur. What was interesting was that she looked familiar. She looked similar to my older sister, Gerri. The girl looked as if she were in her early thirties. The distinct difference between her and my older sister was their hair color. This girl had slightly lighter brown hair compared to my older sister's darker brown.

It then occurred to me that this was my younger sister, Pricilla Brenda. She had passed away when she was only a few days old, and I was a toddler then. My sister was so elated to see me, and I believe she was there to greet me.

I do believe that God sent her to meet me and comfort me. Nothing was said, but our emotions spoke for themselves. She drew closer to me with outstretched arms as I, too, raised my arms to meet her. My heart was filled with love as I imagined my first hug from a sister I had never known.

Then, as soon as we were close to embracing each other,

My mind took me to a different place.

The next thing I knew; I was on an abandoned ship or large boat. Not seeing anyone in sight, I assumed I was alone.

I was lying on the ship's bow and could see and hear waves crashing. As I peered around, I noticed the boat was not in the ocean but beached on what seemed like a deserted island. I decided to explore my surroundings. I raised myself from where I had been resting and entered the interior of my present home. The first area I found was a ballroom. From the smaller size of the room, I guessed that the ship was not a cruise ship, but a large yacht came to mind. As I glanced around, I noticed the room had been set up for some type of party. The tables were decorated with elegant white linens, and sparkling glasses were placed in front of each table setting. I suspected the china was expensive and only used for special occasions. The windows were decorated with frilly, fancy curtains. The tables were arranged around a small dance floor, and a small stage was set up for entertainment.

I walked around the ship trying to find someone, but as I suspected, it seemed as if I were alone. Strangely, it occurred to me that I knew something about the history of this boat.

Somewhere in my memories, I recalled a story about a musician, a guitar player, and his sister, a singer, in their small group. The two siblings had been the main entertainers on board, traveling around the world on this boat. Somehow they died while on tour, and they were cursed to haunt and roam the ship in a spirit-like world. I also recalled that anyone stranded on this ship was also cursed.

I felt an overwhelming sense of loneliness as I realized I might be cursed to remain in my new prison. I returned to the boat's bow and crumbled to the hard wood floor. As I contemplated that my fate may very well be confined to this ghost ship, depression began to set in.

Suddenly, when I finally resigned to knowing I was alone, a young lady appeared at the edge of the bow. I could not see her face clearly, but I knew she was a Hispanic woman. She was small in stature, and from her uniform, I wondered if she had something to do with the medical field. Her outfit was somewhat different than I had been used to seeing in the hospital. She was dressed in what seemed like what an astronaut might wear in space. On her head, she had a helmet made of what seemed like plastic or white cloth. To protect her face, she wore a clear plastic shield. I also noticed a tube protruding from the back of her headgear to a box that was fastened to her waist. The rest of her medical scrubs were navy or dark blue, contrasting with the green normally used by hospital employees where I was admitted.

How she was dressed reminded me of the medical personnel in the movie Outbreak, a medical thriller about a monkey that infected a small town with a deadly virus. The outfit was similar, but in the movie, the uniforms were white, and this woman's attire was blue.

Being curious, I stood up and walked toward her. When I was near, she said, "Mr. Mondragon, I'm here to draw some of your blood. This will only take a minute."

My first thought was that her request had been unusual. Why would this woman want my blood? She took my hand and made a small slit on one of my fingers with some kind of instrument. A small river of blood flowed out of the wound as she captured the flow inside a small oversized vial. I looked down at my hand as I felt the stinging pain generating up my arm. I began to wonder if this woman really knew what she was doing. Was she harming me more than she was helping?

I remember thinking this can't be real. Could this woman belong to some secretive organization that did not belong to a hospital? Even though in my present state of mind, I was not aware I was in the hospital or the circumstances leading up to my stay, I still was aware that this woman was not a hospital employee. Suddenly, after drawing my blood and as quickly as she appeared, she miraculously disappeared before my eyes like some Las Vegas magic act. Her disappearance was followed by a shift in the atmosphere.

A mist began to appear, along with a dense fog. While I was being swallowed up by the tendrils of the fog substance,

My mind took me to a different place.

The next thing I remember was inside an examination room in what seemed like a university setting. The examination room was adjacent to or inside a dormitory. Maybe my mind took me there because my house is located right next to a university. I remember sitting in a chair and noticed two men dressed in hospital uniforms. My first impression of these two individuals was that they resembled scientists more than hospital staff. Both men wore face masks, making it difficult to see their faces. Although, one of the men had a distinctive, well-groomed beard. This man was working at a laptop typing in information.

As I peered around the room, I noticed clear bags hanging from what seemed like clothes hangers. It was then that I heard laughter, music, and boisterous noise coming from what I assumed was a frat party taking place in an adjoining room. I turned my attention back to the two men, who seemed to be creating some kind of drug that was delivered in some type of mist. For some reason, I assumed this drug was being prepared for the partygoers next door.

The two men approached me and placed a face mask on me. The drug they were making suddenly created a mist, which began undulating around my head like a snake weaving around my head to strike. I wondered if I was being used as a guinea pig to test their new creation, and if so, what was its intention.

I don't recall smelling or tasting anything when I was exposed to this drug. All I remember is seeing the mist every time I breathed in and out.

I had the feeling that this misted drug came in a variety of flavors. However, I was given it without the flavoring. Then, somehow I knew what the drug was all about. The drug, with its flavoring mist, was intended to give people a sense of euphoria, peace, and relaxation that could make the person feel as if they were cleansed. The drug also contained all-natural flavors that were not harmful to the body and contained all legal ingredients. I also understood the drug was administered by inhaling it through the nose.

With the amount of finished product, the two student scientists had made, I was sure there was plenty for the partygoers in the next room. I was a bit astounded by their ingenuity, thinking they were probably going to revolutionize the drug world with their invention, Fructose. Since the drug contained all safe, natural ingredients, it could potentially stop illegal drug use worldwide.

The two men gathered their Fructose as they prepared to leave for the frat party.

Somehow I knew I was not allowed to leave the room. As they left the room,

My mind took me to a different place.

The next place my mind took me to was what seemed like my backyard. I looked around, and everything seemed vaguely familiar. I noticed a wooden trap door secretly hidden beneath the sand and loose dirt as I peered around. Being adventurous, I decided to see where the door led, hoping it would answer my questions about where I actually had ended up. I opened the door and noticed a small flight of stairs. I cautiously inched my way down into whatever was waiting for me.

I found myself in what seemed like a basement when I reached the bottom. The single room was set up like a classroom for children. If I ventured to guess, I would say the children ranged in age from eleven to about thirteen. At first glance, I was intrigued by how the learning was supposedly taking place. Instead of using textbooks and laptops, the children appeared to be texting each other or their instructor on their smartphones.

I decided to explore my surroundings further. I inched my way into the classroom, and suddenly I caught the attention of a young girl. When she approached me, my first impression was that she was polite and friendly, as she asked me to have a seat. Then, her demeanor changed. She said to me with a frown, "I'm concerned that you might be in trouble for being here."

It was then that I noticed the classroom's instructor. He was a man that seemed to be around in his late fifties. He was a very intimidating man with piercing black eyes and thick eyebrows. If he had been an actor, he would easily play the part of a mob boss or a drug cartel leader.

He stood in the front of the classroom as if he had the children in some kind of trance. When the instructor noticed my presence, he said in a deep, menacing voice, "Since you entered my class, you are required to obey all of my instructions."

I felt like goosebumps suddenly erupted up and down my arms. Had I discovered some sort of underground society?

The scene reminded me of a movie I once watched called Village of the Damned. It was a movie about a dozen or so children that were born on the same day during a town-wide blackout. It was hinted the children were not of this world and were sent to destroy the world.

Every time the teacher spoke, I felt as if he was trying to hypnotize the children and me, attempting to control our minds. I knew I had to leave at that instant. Otherwise, I would become a shell of a person controlled by this villainous monster. I inched my way backward, looking for the stairs and the trap door to leave this place.

I had reached the stairs when I heard his voice behind me. "From this point on, you are indebted to me. Remember this. I own you!" he bellowed.

I rushed up the stairs, eager to leave the underground nightmare. When I was out of the basement, I was thankful to breathe the fresh air. I looked around to examine the building that I thought was my home. In my state of mind, I was sure this building was my home, but it looked more like a medical building than a residence. It had suddenly become a three-story building, and on its third level, I noticed a light in a room. Defying logic as only dreams are capable of doing, I was able to look inside the third-story room as if I were on the ground floor.

I peered inside the room and saw myself standing in the room wearing a yellow hospital gown. What was different than I expected was the length of my hair. It was long and cascaded down my shoulders, similar to the length I had. I kept it when I was a teenager. I noticed a hospital bed and a tray next to my younger self. I knew I was standing, but I felt myself in the hospital room was not doing well. The scene was difficult to witness, so I made a conscious effort to look away. As I turned,

My mind took me to a different place.

8

When I was aware of my surroundings, I was sitting in a strange hospital room. A television was located in the upper corner of a wall. On the television screen was what seemed like a lady news anchor in a small square in the far corner of the screen. The channel selection on the television set reminded me of the type used in the late seventies or early eighties. It had several colors to indicate the type of channel broadcasting, such as blue for news, green for movies, etc. I listened intensely as the woman was reporting about a new craving sensation called Fruitose. I looked around the room and noticed it was full of medical equipment. Oddly, the equipment was all made of plastic. While examining my surroundings, I was aware that light blue hoses, which may have been electrical tubing, were protruding from the equipment. There were also several metal tables in the room, and on top were what seemed like a slew of old Nintendo game consoles. On the front of the consoles were red, yellow, blue, and green buttons.

Suddenly, the hospital room went dark. It was not as if someone had turned out the lights but as if my subconscious mind was reacting to the next part of my dream. Through the darkness, a face began materializing, and he was in the middle of teaching a class to children. The first thing I noticed about him was the evil aura that surrounded his body. The evil man turned to me and said, "I need to ask you some questions and settle some debts." He had some old film strips he wanted to show me. Oddly, the images from the film strips appeared without any machine to project them.

The first film he wanted to show me was of an older gentleman standing next to a shiny, glowing horse. The man, possibly a Hispanic, had a dark complexion and was wearing a white cowboy hat. The man's hair was long, possibly shoulder length, and he wore it in a single braid.

My dream shifted to an image of what looked like either a black or Hispanic person's rear end that was unattached to his torso. I recall being confused until the evil man said, "It is your job to attach the man's derriere to make him whole."

I wondered if the detached man was the same elderly gentleman next to the glowing horse. The evil man added, "If you fail in this task, then you will lose the deed to your house."

I guess in my mind, I was concerned about losing my house, and I thought about how hard it could be to stitch the man back together. I didn't wonder why this man had picked me to do this task other than his attempt to control me.

My mind took me to a different place.

I was then whisked away to another place. I landed in the middle of what seemed like a movie set. I wasn't sure if I was the director or possibly a producer, but I definitely was a person in charge. The movie that was being produced was called "Pikachu Bonsai ." I was sure of this because I saw a movie poster nearby. On the poster, there was a big red apple with a slice that had been taken out of the middle.

A few apple seeds were visible in the center of the apple. A bee was flying just right off the apple. In the background were tall skyscraper buildings and numerous high-priced cars. On each side of the poster, a young man and woman were standing and dressed in military garb. A young Asian boy stood in the middle of the military couple. I believe the boy's name was "Pikachu Bonsai."

The plot of the movie was about Chad and Lisa, two members of an elite military unit that despised each other. While on a mission, they rescued this little orphan boy. They both fell in love with this boy but still couldn't get along with each other. I remember plenty of car chases and wrecks in the movie, which reminded me of the Fast and the Furious movies.

The fruitose craze was an integral part of the movie. Most of the characters in the movie were addicted to the fruitose substance. The problem with taking too much of the substance was not dangerous, but the residue was difficult to dislodge from a person's gums and teeth.

This fruitose substance ruined a very expensive car on the set, and the cost to restore the car would be more than what it was worth. So, I decided to crash it in the movie.

As the movie plot progressed, the couple's love for the orphan boy grew, and their dislike for each other diminished. At the movie's end, the couple finally realized they had fallen in love and mutually agreed to adopt the orphan boy.

Being a movie executive, I had a plush office at the top of a high-rise building, a building that was similar to the Seattle Space Needle. I recall the office had large windows that allowed me to look into my surroundings for miles. There was glass all around, so I could see above and below me. At the conclusion of filming, I asked the couple, Chad and Lisa, to my office to hand them their paychecks. When they arrived, I began feeling sapped of energy, and my breathing was labored. I was concerned I would not be able to stand for much longer. Before I knew I was going to pass out, I advised my guests that I needed to lie down.

My mind took me to a different place.

When I was aware of my surroundings, I knew I was back on the ship. I remember feeling alone and extremely depressed. I plopped myself back on the ship's bow, listening to the roar of the waves crashing. What happened next was very peculiar.

I felt as if I were reliving a past event, which reminded me of the movie Groundhog Day. In the movie, Bill Murray, the main actor, keeps reliving the same day over and over. As with a past dream segment, a nurse appeared from the fog in some type of medical space suit garb, saying she had come to draw blood from me. When she completes her task, she miraculously disappears back into the fog. After she is gone,

My mind took me to a different place.

Next, I found myself in the same medical building that I thought previously was my house. I peered around at my surroundings and decided I was in some kind of lobby. To the left of me, I noticed what seemed like some kind of check-in desk. When I turned to my right, I saw several rows of tables, which I assumed was a cafeteria, and next to the wall tucked inside an alcove were various vending machines. Ahead of me, there was an area that I believed was a waiting and reception area. Several matching couches and chairs were available for seating, along with end tables that were covered with an assortment of magazines. On the far wall hung several plaques, which I guessed were tributes to some city officials.

I took a seat on one of the couches that faced the plaques. Suddenly, I looked up and saw a bright ray of light above the plaques in the far right-hand corner. Then, what I believed was coming from the center of the light was a clicking sound, which sounded similar to the clicking you hear from your cell phone when someone is texting you on messenger.

I watched as the light slowly began sliding down the wall. I felt fear and, at the same time, curiosity as the phenomena unfolded before my eyes. Then, all logic drained away as a voice bellowed from the ray of light in a sinister, raspy tone. "Larry, Larry, you are a liar. Larry, you are a liar."

I wasn't sure what it all meant, but I wondered if this voice belonged to the same man that was attempting to trick me into giving him the deed to my house.

As I was pondering this idea,

My mind took me to a different place.

I was elated to have left the medical building, but my dream took me to another building. I was on the top floor of a tall building and found myself lying on my stomach. I glanced around at my surroundings, which was difficult with the position I found myself in, but I managed to see a window open. I knew for certain because I could feel the breeze sneaking in through the window. The breeze was neither hot nor cold nor mild nor strong, but it whipped just enough to reach me.

Just then, I noticed joyful laughter and commotion coming from the next room. I assumed a party was taking place.

I attempted to catch a glimpse in that direction, and to my surprise, I found the door to the next room wide open. I watched as a crowd of people had some kind of drink and took turns inhaling the new craze, Fruitose. I recognized one of the men from my prior dream in the college dorm. He was one of the student scientists manufacturing the Fruitose. He was working on his laptop near a table filled with fluid-filled bags. From what I could see, he was mixing the Fruitose for the partygoers.

I tried to move from the position I found myself in, but I was unsuccessful. All I could do was watch from my vantage point and listen. I recall feeling anxious because Mary, my wife, was expected to visit me. I missed her greatly, which added to my feeling of loneliness. My weariness was overwhelming, causing me to nod off regularly. However, whenever I awakened, I would frantically search to see if Mary had arrived. Unfortunately, I was disappointed when I found myself alone. When I was contemplating my present dilemma,

My mind took me to a different place.

The whole world, as I knew it, had changed. For some odd reason, I wondered if the changes to the future had to do with the rise of crime. The human race has evolved to the extent that we have colonized a variety of different planets. Not only had we expanded our living capabilities, but we had perfected space travel. Traveling between the planets had become as fast as traveling from one city to another. The housing on these planets was generally apartment complexes, which I recall were called pods.

As I was soaking in my new surroundings, I witnessed how the entertainment industry had evolved. Bands of musicians of different genres entertained others by traveling in spacecrafts from venue to venue. Their spacecrafts traveled through space, lighting the skies like discos lights from the nineteen seventies. When the spacecraft, with the band of musicians inside, reached its destination, they merely opened up their craft, jumped out and started performing. The spacecraft provided a multitude of lighting possibilities and housed the speaker systems. These concerts were usually held at the apartment complexes and often directly to specific households.

It wasn't long before I began reminiscing about the bands I remember listening to and performing their music when I, too, performed in bands when I was younger. I recall bands such as; the Brothers Johnson, the Commodores, the Barclays, and the O'Jays. As I was reminiscing about these times,

My mind took me to a different place.

I opened my eyes and found myself lying in my own bed in my house. Through the darkness, I could hear these high-pitched, piercing screams echoing somewhere out in the neighborhood. My first thought that came to mind was whatever was making that noise had to be evil. I lifted myself from my bed and looked out into the darkness. Out in the street, roaming the neighborhood, was an animal the size of a large dog. Even though it resembled a dog, it was more beast than canine. It was black and gray with wet, matted fur as if it had come directly out of the sewer. When it screamed and howled, it revealed rows of yellow, razor-sharp teeth, which reminded me of an alligator or a crocodile. Also, when the beast opened its mouth, a plume of fog and mist erupted into the air like a cloud of gnats had been released.

I suddenly realized that this beast was the culprit for spreading diseases worldwide. His mission was to infect humankind with whatever virus he was carrying. The beast didn't need to attack but merely spew out the disease into the neighborhoods.

I then understood why the dreadful screams the beast was making sounded so familiar. The same sounds were coming from my chest when I had trouble breathing. Could this be the beast living inside of me? As I contemplated this revelation,

My mind took me to a different place.

9

When I was finally aware of my surroundings, I knew I was back in the medical building that I once thought was my house. I was standing in the same area where previously I had seen the ray of light and the ticking sound coming from high in the wall above the plaques of public officials. I still remembered the raspy, evil voice that had spoken to me that I was a liar.

This time there was a lady present along with a young girl. The girl looked like the same girl I had met in the classroom basement. The same girl that was polite enough to offer me a seat, but at the same time concerned that I shouldn't have been there. Somehow I knew that Mary, my wife, had spoken to the lady and was able to convince her that I needed her help. I also wondered if this lady was the wife or ex-wife of the class instructor in the basement. This man could also be connected to the voice behind the shadow.

I believed the lady had brought the girl to fight for my soul and to convince the man in the light to leave me alone. I wondered if the child's innocence was needed to fight the evil the man possessed. I once again felt an overwhelming sense that this evil man was attempting to blackmail me for the deed to my house.

As I heard and witnessed before, I heard the clicking sound, and then a ray of light appeared on the ceiling. Like a panther stalking its prey, the light slowly made its way down the wall. After about halfway down the wall, the apparition froze. A dense fog had enveloped the light reminding me of a lighthouse near the shore of a tumultuous tide banging against the rocks. Then, I heard that raspy, evil voice saying, "Larry, Larry, you are a liar."

My head began to spin as I was petrified with fear. How could I battle such a being when he had the capability of controlling my very inner being? I knew if I stood for very much longer, I would faint. I quickly looked around and plopped myself onto the nearest couch. The weakness began spreading from the top of my head to the smallest of my toes.

Then the girl began shouting at the man in the fog, "He is not a liar! You are the liar! Leave him alone!"

The man seemed to ignore the girl as he concentrated his efforts on me. Like a mantra, he kept repeating to me, "Larry, Larry, you are a liar. Larry, Larry, you are a liar."

The girl was also relentlessly defending me with every fiber in her small body, screaming repeatedly, "He is not a liar! Leave him alone!"

With my energy draining with every passing moment, I listened to the man, and the girl vie back and forth until,

My mind took me to a different place.

As I became aware of my surroundings, I found myself back in the tall building where the two student scientists were making Fruitose and a frat party was taking place in an adjoining room. However, this time I found myself on the basement floor. As I had been on occasion, I was lying on my stomach and finding it difficult to move from my position. With some effort, I could move my hands around a bit.

I could peer around at my surroundings, noticing a door that was ajar. Through the small slit of the door, I could see what appeared to be one of the spaceships used by musical performers to travel from house to house. I wondered if this building was used to build these spacecrafts.

It was then that I noticed the people in the room. The group was all chanting or praying, and it seemed as if they were encouraging me to get up. All the group members were taking turns inhaling the fruitose. They were all holding candles as they continued to chant or pray.

I suddenly felt as if Mary, my wife, was standing right next to me, but I was unable to see her. I attempted to move my hands so that I could actually reach out and touch her. I began to feel frustrated, and the frustration quickly turned to anger as I could not find my wife. I missed her greatly, and I needed her by my side more than ever. It was then that,

My mind took me to a different place.

Well, I was back on the ship again, but this time the feeling of loneliness and being so far from everyone had followed me from the building's basement. As before, I plopped myself down on the ship's bow to rest. It was then that I began to hear voices. I wasn't sure if the voices were real or just part of my imagination. Nevertheless, the voices were explaining to me that people with asthma or chronic diseases would end up on this ship.

A fog-like mist started to materialize. Tendrils of fog-like fingers inched their way around the ship as if looking for food to devour. From out of this environment, a young man appeared. He was wearing a blue gown and appeared to be blowing into a clear tube. He approached me and said several times, "I'm here for you."

My impression of the man, as he continually breathed into the tube, was that he was arrogant. I also felt as if he was trying his best to impress me. Although, no matter what he did, I was not impressed. Yet, on the other hand, I wondered if he had come to teach me how to breathe into the tube.

I began to feel anxious and clammy. Sweat dripped down my face as I knew my body temperature was rising. It was then,

My mind took me to a different place.

I ended up in a forest with beautiful flowers blooming all around and tall trees with green branches reaching the mossy undergrowth. In the distance, I noticed a small log cabin, enticing travelers to take advantage of its warm fireplace, as enticing as the gingerbread house in the fairy tale Hansel and Gretel.

As I was taking on the scenery of my new environment, I was given a message by some unseen force, telling me that there was going to be a showing of the last picture show or movie. Somehow I was able to tap into the minds of all people, and like me, they were unsure what this meant. I wondered if we, as humankind, had run out of ideas for movies; therefore, after this last movie is shown, no others will follow. There were some people that believed the showing of the last picture show would also be the end of the world.

Not knowing if the showing of this movie could be the end of humankind forced me to reflect on my own life. Like a movie of my own life, I saw myself as a young boy. In my first vision, I was riding my bike, an activity I loved to do. I would ride for hours, pretending I was riding all over the country, exploring cities and countries I only dreamed about in textbooks. I remember me and my brother, Floyd, making a high jump in our backyard and practicing our high jump skills until it was dark. When it would rain, puddles developed near the highway where I grew up, and Floyd and I would spend the day catching tadpoles in these makeshift ponds.

My next vision took me to a time when I would practice on my guitar, listen to music on a record player, and then duplicate on my guitar what I heard on the records. Then, I saw myself playing the guitar in dance bands with various musicians. I couldn't distinguish any of my band members because their faces were a blur. My vision shifted to a time when I was riding in the back of a flatbed truck playing music with a band during a parade for the Colorado State Fair. A large crowd had gathered on both sides of the street, cheering for the parade participants.

I was then reminded of my time when I was into running. It was not only exercising time for me, but I found myself enjoying the adrenaline rush as I pushed myself for miles. I ran so far at times that I could look back over my shoulder and see the city of Pueblo in the distance.

As I was in the middle of reflecting on my own past, my dream changed considerably. I had almost forgotten about the message that was given to me about the last picture show. I returned from my reminiscing to the forest with the beautiful flowers. Then, I noticed a clearing had opened up in the forest. I approached the clearing and noticed an enclosure that was octagon shaped with carefully set flagstone on its flooring. A black, rod-iron fence encircled the enclosure with four gates at each of its corners. Flagstone walkways also led up to each of these gates. The walkways extended far out into the forest, which reminded me of the yellow brick road in the *Wizard of Oz*. I would not have been surprised if Munchkins appeared to welcome me into Munchkin land.

Instead of Munchkins, four figures appeared on each of the walkways. They began their slow march down the flagstone walkway as if they were robots. Their jerky, flaying motions reminded me if they were running on batteries that were close to expiring.

As they drew closer to the octagon enclosure, I was able to recognize who they were. The first was singer, songwriter, and entertainer Michael Jackson. He wore his signature costume, black and white, wide, brimmed hat, shiny, sparkling jacket, and single white glove.

The next figure was Edward Scissorhands. He was easy to recognize with his black attire, painted face, and the long scissors protruding from his hands. On the third walkway, a figure that was recognizable by most that ever watched television, the Scarecrow from the Wizard of OZ. He was obvious with his straw hat, floppy physique, and straw sticking out from various areas of his body. The last figure approaching the octagon was another movie icon, Beetlejuice. He was easily recognized with his stripped clothing, white, wild hair, and ghost-like make-up.

I watched as these four giants of the movie screen made their way down each of their respective paths. Each of these characters didn't look real, but more as if they were puppets or robots. As I watched, mesmerized by the scene before me, I wondered if this march had something to do with the last picture show. It seemed as if each figure was competing to get to the center of the octagon first.

I didn't know for sure if the winner to the center won the right to star in the last picture show or if the winner represented the last picture show.

As I watched anxiously to see what would happen when a winner finally reached the center, their pace seemed to slow. Their arms and legs flayed about as if a master puppeteer was controlling their movements. Then, as they drew closer to each of their respective gates, a horrifying thought came to mind. If one of the figures won the contest, could this mean the end of the world?

As the four figures found their way only inches away from the gates, in slow motion, they each raised their hands to touch the rod-iron doors, and I gasped. Sweat was rolling down the side of my face, not from heat but from the anticipation of what may follow. As each figure placed their hands on the gates, they froze as if time stood still. It was then,

My mind took me to a different place.

I found myself back in a hospital room in a hospital bed. The room seemed bigger than I had expected. It had space for several beds, even though my bed was the only one I could see. This dream seemed to be different from my previous dreams. It reminded me much like the time being stuck between the dream world and awakening. Nevertheless, I felt it necessary to find out about my surroundings. I tried to look around, but my movements were restrained. The first thing I noticed was a slight, cool breeze washing over my body. I tried to cover my body to stay warm, but I couldn't manage to move my hands. I wondered if I could be paralyzed.

To the side of me, I noticed a nurse working at a table. It looked as if she was preparing some kind of food in a bowl. For some odd reason, I felt as if she was preparing something for me. I also noticed another person putting up what looked like cards in the window facing out into the hallway.

The cards, which could have been birthday cards, and the bowl of food, could very well be preparations for some kind of celebration for me. Yet, I knew it was not my birthday. The thought of getting something to eat was enticing; I couldn't remember the last time I had eaten.

Seeing all the movement of several people in my room and a stream of people in the hallway, I decided to pretend as if I were still asleep. If it was some type of surprise, I didn't want to give away that I knew.

Being as quiet as possible, my mind began to wander. With the movement in the hallway and what seemed like laundry baskets being pushed somewhere, I wondered if a laundry facility was nearby. I played possum for what seemed like an eternity, having doubts about a celebration. I began to feel anxious and wavering on the idea that maybe I should ask someone what was actually going on. After a considerable time, I found myself tired and in need of rest.

Whatever was going on, it could wait till the morning. Before long, I found myself falling into a deep sleep.

The next thing I remember; I was screaming in pain. The room seemed in total darkness, and I found myself screaming, "It hurts! It hurts!"

I heard a female voice saying to me, "Larry, Larry, stop. There is nothing going on that is causing you any pain!"

I ignored her voice and continued to scream, "It hurts! It hurts!"

I was sure the female, who I assumed was a hospital caregiver, was wrong. Something was causing me pain. It was then that I realized I was no longer in a medically induced coma. Suddenly, I felt pain in my head, like a wooden vise with thick chains was attached to my brain, and someone was slowly cranking it closed.

Then, through the darkness, I heard a male's voice, which I assumed was speaking to the woman, "You make the call."

I had somehow awakened from the medically induced coma and struggled to extract the tubes from my mouth and nose that were keeping me alive while I was in a coma. It is considered rare for a person to awake from a medically induced come on their own without some type of medical assistance. Yet, there was the question of whether my body had healed sufficiently during the coma to battle the virus within me while I was now awake. Fortunately, the medical staff that was monitoring my progress had decided not to return me to the medically induced coma. This was the point that my fight with the virus took a turn for the better.

I remember waking up being very confused, as if part of my mind was still in the dream world. I recall a male nurse entering my room and saying someone wanted to speak with me. I looked around as if in a fog and saw my wife, Mary, and my daughter, Molly, looking at me and speaking to me. I learned later that I was conversing with them on a tablet, but in my state of mind, I thought I saw a section of the wall or ceiling open up, and they appeared to me in some kind of cloud. Nevertheless, I was so happy to see them. I was unable to speak, but all I wanted to do was listen to their voices.

After a bit, I didn't know what was real and what wasn't. If this was real, I didn't want my family to see me like this. I recall turning to the nurse and asking him to stop whatever was happening. I needed time to clear my head and make sense of what was happening. If I had truly awakened from my dream world, then why did I feel as if I still couldn't discern what was real and what was made up in my mind?

10

Over the next few days, I struggled with reality, but as each day passed, I became more aware of my surroundings and what actually happened to me. I discovered I was in an induced coma and on a ventilator for sixteen days. During that time, I was given Fentanyl, Propofol, along with several respiratory treatments. Knowing I was on these powerful drugs helped me to understand my state of confusion when I awakened. I had been told by the doctors that even after I had awakened and taken myself off the ventilator, they were still unsure whether I would survive. I had beaten the odds of recovery for those who were placed in medically induced comas.

After some debate among the doctors, a feeding tube was placed in my nose. With some sustenance, it seemed as if my strength was returning. However, it took nearly five days for my mind to function normally. I believed that I had enough strength to at least go to the bathroom on my own. I requested a nurse to do so when she laughed and said I wouldn't even be able to take two steps. I disagreed with her, thinking I had enough strength to do so. Later that day, I was visited by two orderlies that were from physical therapy. They had come to get me to start walking. It was then that I realized my body would not cooperate. It was a chore to even lift my arms. My first task was to get out of bed and sit in a chair, a task I could not do without their assistance. I learned I could not even stand on my own. My body felt as if I weighed a ton. With their help and the use of a walker, I managed two steps. My physical therapy session was finished for the day. I felt exhausted. I was also in shock as I wondered if this was going to be what my life was going to be like.

I was still connected to several machines, and my breathing was still labored. I spent a lot of time in bed with my thoughts. I thanked God regularly for saving my life. Since I had time on my hands, I spent time with friends and family on social media. I was overwhelmed by all the comments and prayers that were posted. I felt blessed that I had so many people that cared and worried about me. I also felt extremely sad for what my family and friends had to go through, not knowing I would awaken from my coma.

How and why I survived is still a mystery to me. However, I need to mention something that I feel is important and worth considering. During the time that I was arousing from my coma, a short distance away in a park, my wife and a group of friends had met for a prayer vigil on my behalf. At the time they were praying, I was pulling out the life-saving tubes and awakening from my coma. Was this divine intervention or just a coincidence?

My wife, Mary, was at my side during all that I went through. Physically, she was restricted from the hospital because of Covid protocols, but I knew she was only a phone call away. I also knew how difficult this must have been for her, and for this reason, I wanted her to tell you in her own words the difficulties she personally had to go through.

"It was the worst nightmare of my life! I never dreamed anything like this would happen to our family. My husband is one of the strongest people I know. I couldn't believe this could happen to him. We had just moved into a new house. It wasn't too long after we moved in that the virus began spreading worldwide. At first, we thought it would be like the flu, but the mortality rate among those who caught the virus was much higher. Hearing about all the people dying daily was heart-wrenching. Soon after the virus began spreading, local, national and worldwide restrictions were imposed.

"Mask-wearing in public became the norm, and we ventured out only for work and to get necessary supplies. Larry was sent home for a short while but then returned to work, while I, on the other hand, never stopped working until I caught the virus. The virus had been going strong for several months, and thankfully it seemed as if we had avoided getting sick.

"Then, one Saturday, Larry came home from work saying he wasn't feeling well. He was sick all weekend and called off work on Monday. According to his work's protocol, he was told he had to test negative for Covid before he was allowed to return to work. After I got off work, I took him to urgent care, where he tested positive. They also tested me, and I was positive. Since our daughter lived at home, Urgent Care advised me to call our daughter to come in and also get tested. Unfortunately, she also tested positive. As a result, we all had to quarantine.

"At first, Molly and I were very sick, and Larry kept telling us to get up and eat something. His symptoms seemed to be on the mild to moderate side. However, after about four days, Molly and I started to feel better, but Larry took a turn for the worse. He wouldn't eat or drink anything; all he wanted to do was sleep. We encouraged him to get up and eat something or at least drink some fluids. He refused, saying everything tasted like metal.

"His birthday was coming up, so we ordered cherry pie. It was his favorite dessert. I knew something terrible was wrong when he refused to eat a bite. The next morning he said he thought it best to go to the ER. I drove him there but was not allowed in because I was still in quarantine. Sitting in the car and watching him go in alone was so hard. I went home expecting to receive a call to come and pick him up. But instead, I got a call saying they had admitted him to the hospital. Since his oxygen levels were in his forties, which were dangerously low, he would be admitted into the Intensive Care Unit. The news really scared me. What if he hadn't gone in?

"The next few months were so hard. After he had been in Intensive Care for a while, I got a phone call from him saying they were going to put him on a ventilator. I was shocked I didn't know he was that sick. He said he was calling to say goodbye to the kids and me and to say that he loved us all. I refused to say goodbye but said I would see you later. He said ok, I'll see you later. I could tell he was confused by what was about to happen as I was.

"It was so hard while he was on the ventilator not being able to go see him or at least call and talk to him. Molly and I prayed for him constantly. Many of our family members and friends also said they were praying for him. I called the hospital at least three times a day when there was a shift change so I could talk to the next nurse for updates. I knew they were busy, but they took the time to give me updates. Most of the time, I was told there was no change. I dreaded talking to the doctors because they always sounded so frustrated. They kept telling me about a new thing they would try, but they didn't sound like they believed it would work.

"I cried and prayed so much for God to save him. I wasn't ready to let him go. We still had so many plans. He is my best friend, and I couldn't think of living life without him. I tried to keep the rest of the family up to date on what the doctors were saying. Yet, I didn't have a lot of answers to their questions. Even the doctors didn't really know what to say. I received a few phone calls asking if I wanted them to make him comfortable because there was not much more they could do. I said no. I didn't want to be selfish, but I couldn't see letting him go if his brain, heart, and other organs were good. I wanted to keep trying to save him. I knew in my heart God would save him.

"So we continued every day calling and checking on him. The nurses were great and gave me hope, but he still wasn't improving much. I received another phone call from a doctor while I was at work. The doctor asked again if I wanted them to just make him comfortable because there was not nothing else they could do. I asked her what would happen if she took him off the ventilator. She said he would have to go on a trachea, which was a breathing tube in the throat, and he will have to be admitted to a nursing home. I listened, but I wasn't quite sure what decision to make. She realized I had a big decision to make and politely asked me to think about it and let her know. I hung up the phone and asked to go home from work to think and pray.

"We, as a family and friends, had a prayer meeting that weekend at a park near the hospital. A pastor friend of ours joined us. As my daughter and I left the prayer meeting, I received a phone call from one of the nurses at the hospital. She asked if I was driving and if I was to pull over and call her back. Since I had been on the road, I pulled over nervously, and with my hands shaking, I called the nurse back. I had no idea what the conversation would entail, but the worst-case scenarios passed through my mind.

"I called on the speakerphone so Molly could also hear the conversation. The nurse answered and began stuttering a bit, saying she didn't know how to explain. Finally, she blurted out that Larry had awakened from his coma and pulled out his ventilator tube. She seemed distressed, as if it was her fault, saying she had tried to put it back in, but Larry wouldn't let her. She apologized several times.

"Molly and I cried and laughed at the same time because we knew our prayers were being answered. I was sure the nurse thought we were crazy. She politely asked if I was mad. Through my laughter and tears, I said of course not. I see this as a good thing.

"I knew then that Larry was going to be okay. I realized that after 16 days in a coma and hooked up to a ventilator, his recovery would be long and difficult. Nevertheless, I was prepared to be at his side throughout his recovery. In the following days and weeks, he kept improving little by little. It was a miracle. He had to go through several surgeries associated with bed sores, spent numerous rehab appointments, and he still struggles with keeping his oxygen levels at acceptable levels. Even though, at times, he is dependent upon a portable oxygen unit, and he is still with us. God saw us through it all and gave us the strength needed to keep fighting for him. God saved my husband's life, and I will forever be grateful."

My daughter, Molly, went through her own ordeal with the virus but also had to endure the hardship of not knowing what could happen to her father. For this reason, I felt it was pertinent to add to my story a small part of her journey during this difficult time in our lives.

"I always thought my dad was invincible. I sometimes took him for granted because I believed that nothing bad would ever happen to him. I never thought there would come a day when he would be gone. He is not only my best friend, but he has always been a person I look up to. This made what happened to him so much worse for me because I was faced with the reality that the virus could take him away from me.

"In order to understand the situation, let me start from the beginning.

"In 2020, I was working at Subway. Covid had begun spreading earlier in the year. I was working to save up money to return to school sometime in the future. I remember hearing that the virus seemed to be slowing its progression, but a mask mandate was still in place. I was pleased that the lockdown mandate was easing up, and I was finally able to get out and do things.

"Since my parents were older, I made sure to follow all the precautions so that they would not catch the virus. To compensate, I pretty much kept myself in self-isolation. I usually only went to work and back home. I was also worried that I would catch or spread the disease among my friends, which caused me to visit by phone or social media rather than in person.

"My parents and I had gone seven months' virus free, and I had hoped that we had avoided the virus completely. It was also during this time that I gave my life over to God, which helped me to pour myself into scripture reading and prayer. All was going well until September 21st, 2020, the date of my father's birthday.

"Prior to this time, all three of us had tested positive for Covid, but my mother and I had only mild to moderate symptoms. Since we had to self-isolate, all three of us were at home. That day my dad began to experience symptoms of the virus. My mother and I knew he was not feeling well when he had trouble eating grapes. We decided he needed his rest and encouraged him to drink plenty of fluids.

The next morning when I woke up, my parents were gone. I learned that sometime during the night, my dad's oxygen levels had begun falling dangerously, which required my mother to take him into the emergency room. My mother was not allowed to accompany my dad because she had also tested positive for Covid. My father was admitted to the hospital, and my mother and I spent the next few months unable to visit him. He would call and share with us his daily life in the intensive care unit. Some days he seemed as if he were getting better, then on other days, we weren't sure. This was a difficult time in my life.

"Since his oxygen levels were unstable and his symptoms became severe, the doctors decided to put him on a ventilator. I was asleep when my mother received the call from the hospital. I remember feeling devastated that I hadn't had the chance to tell him that I loved him. The thought came to mind that maybe I could have talked to my dad for the last time.

"I didn't know how to cope with my father's latest development. I was aware that many people had battled with the virus, and those that had to be put on a ventilator, their chances for recovery were diminished greatly. My mom and I were alone to deal with this dilemma, and I had never felt so helpless in my life. Since I had given over my life to Christ, I turned to Him in this difficult time. In the midst of all the questions with no answers, I trusted God to take care of my father. I knew God had a bigger purpose for my dad, and I believed God would get him through this.

"I cried more tears than I thought my body could hold. But through it all, I knew Jesus was comforting me and speaking to me in that still, small voice. When I was in prayer and scripture reading, I was in a safe place and refuge in the midst of the life's storm I was experiencing. I prayed for divine intervention from the Creator, promising to bring my dad back to serving Christ if his life would be saved.

"After my dad was on a ventilator for over a week, it seemed like I was wavering in hope. I felt as if a part of me was missing, and that part could only be filled with my dad's presence. Doctors called my mom and asked her if they could let him go because of his lack of improvement. Yet, my mom was adamant and advised the medical personnel to continue doing everything possible to save his life. We continued to trust in God and believed that my dad would get better.

"There was a prayer meeting for my dad, which my mom and I attended. Several people were at the prayer meeting, and together we pleaded for God to heal my father. We didn't realize that at that time, God was listening to our prayers and working a miracle in my dad's life. A short time later, my mom and I were driving to a store to buy groceries when we received a call from the hospital. Immediately, we were filled with fear and anxiety and started to panic. My mother answered the phone and received news that my dad had awakened and pulled out the tubes to his ventilator by the grace and strength of God.

"The news meant that my dad was going to make it. The doctors were still skeptical about his recovery, but I knew that through the grace of God, his body was healing. Even the doctors could not explain his recovery.

"It's been a long journey since then. I had to quit my job to help at home with my dad. I regularly read scripture to him, and when he regained some strength, we returned going to church as a family. It's been a difficult recovery for my dad, but I know that God has a specific purpose for him. In a recent family visit to Israel, he was baptized in the Jordan River. His faith grows each day as he relies on God's strength and guidance. I pray for whoever is reading this that you know a person is never too far gone from God's healing touch. He makes a way when it seems like all hope is lost. I thank God daily for the grace He has shown my dad and my family. This experience helped me to appreciate life more, and knowing how short our life is on this earth, we must always treat one another with love."

Throughout my life, I've tried to remember to pray for people in need, but I fell short of making those pleas in earnest. I took for granted God's healing power, and at times I may have been a bit skeptical that such power really existed. I've prayed for healing, positive things to happen in their lives, and freedom from financial problems, but I have to ask myself if those prayers were actually heartfelt and based on faith. Since I spend a lot of time on social

Battling the Beast – Through the power of prayer

media platforms, I've witnessed numerous prayer requests and accounts of how those prayers have been answered.

Now that I've experienced first-hand the healing power of God and the power that is available through faith in prayer, my approach to life has changed considerably. If I say now that I will pray for a person, I take that act very seriously. God sends the everyday people in our lives to do his work. I noticed this first-hand from the orderlies that took care of my daily needs, the nurses that watched me each day, and the doctors that made the decisions to save my life. I remember a very special nurse's assistant by the name of Amy that came into my room at the beginning of her shift to visit with me. I recall during those times of confusion, when I would call her by another name, she would tell me who she was and would write her name on the dry-erase board.

Through this experience, I want to be a better person, husband, and father. Jesus Christ comes first in my life and is now the Lord of my household and family. I still have a long journey ahead of healing.

Covid has left me with lung problems that may affect me for the rest of my life. I recall waking up from the coma and going through a diet of liquids, then advancing to a puree diet, and finally to bite-size foods. My strength took several weeks to return. I was taken for a walk in a park near the hospital in physical therapy. I started with a wheelchair and then slowly was able to walk with the use of a walker. The two-block trek usually sapped my energy.

When I was discharged from the hospital, I continued my own physical therapy by practicing walking up and down the stairs. My bedroom was upstairs, and I wanted to make the climb on my own. However, Mary and Molly had to help for several weeks.

My recovery has been grueling, but I am well enough to return to work. I started working part-time, but I am back to a full-time schedule with time. However, there are days that I need to take my portable oxygen pack with me to work.

Recently, my family and I took a tour with some Christian friends to Israel. The experience was phenomenal. We visited sights associated with the birth, life, and crucifixion of Jesus, as well as the tomb where he rose from on Easter Sunday. Knowing that I was able to make this trip, when only months before I didn't know I would ever leave the hospital, was very humbling to me. Not only was the experience spiritual, but it renewed my love for my family and a new appreciation for life. I'm not completely sure why God saved my life, but I am certain that he still has plans for me. I think it's fair to say that my experience with Covid was crippling for my family and me, but as they say, every cloud has a silver lining. Yet, I am grateful to God that he finds me worthy to pass through the fires of difficulty so that I may be purified like gold.

11

Many psychologists, psychiatrists, and spiritual leaders believe we live our lives battling with ourselves about what is wrong and right. How we choose to obey those urgings depends on several factors. Some believe our upbringing and the influence and guidance we receive from our parents, relatives, school teachers, and community leaders determine whether we believe some action is right or wrong. While on the other hand, some believe the ability to determine right or wrong is programmed into our being at the time of our infancy.

I am not advocating either belief, but I wish to believe that maybe there is some truth in both possibilities. I also believe that almost every person enters this world with the innate ability to favor good over evil. The exception to this would be someone with a sociopathic personality. I think it's safe to say that everyone has some kind of internal devise, which many refer to as our consciousness. As we grew older, we were confronted with a host of different decisions, and our conscious told us what was right and wrong. Some believe our ability to know the difference between right and wrong was given to us at birth. Yet, our battle to make the right decisions is a life-long process.

As I reflect on the events of my dreams and visions while in a coma, I wonder if many were connected to strings of memories. Yet, I believe that some of the dreams and visions may have been rooted in some spiritual influence. On the other hand, some were so bizarre that even an expert in the field would have difficulty interpreting their significance.

I believe each reader will have to interpret the events differently depending on their own spiritual and psychological upbringing. Nevertheless, my view of our purpose in life has changed considerably since my illness. Did I flirt with death and live because of my antibodies, or did I live because some cosmic entity determined that my time had not yet expired? I would like to believe that my will to live, my love for my wife, Mary, and my family, also were factored somewhere into that equation.

Did a battle between good and evil occur while I was on the cusp of determining where I would spend my eternity? That's an interesting question that I ask myself often. Nevertheless, I believe that if a battle occurred between the forces of evil and the angels of God, good will conquer evil. I am living proof that God takes care of His children, and for that, I am forever indebted to my family, friends, and, most of all, to my Savior, Jesus Christ.

Made in the USA
Coppell, TX
15 March 2024